ONCE UPON A
CLIMB

ONCE UPON A CLIMB

5 STEPS EVERY DREAMER SHOULD KNOW

JENNIFER A. NIELSEN

SHADOW
MOUNTAIN
PUBLISHING

Visit us at shadowmountain.com

Library of Congress Cataloging-in-Publication Data

Names: Nielsen, Jennifer A., author.
Title: Once upon a climb: 5 steps every dreamer should know / Jennifer A. Nielsen.
Description: Salt Lake City: Shadow Mountain, [2023] | Includes bibliographical references. | Summary: "#1 New York Times bestselling author Jennifer A. Nielsen shares an inspirational message about the 5 steps that can help anyone with a dream achieve their goal"—Provided by publisher.
Identifiers: LCCN 2023020965 | ISBN 9781639931729 (hardback)
Subjects: LCSH: Self-actualization (Psychology) | Self-realization. | BISAC: SELF-HELP / Motivational & Inspirational | LCGFT: Self-help publications.
Classification: LCC BF637. S4 N535 2023 | DDC 158.1—dc23/eng/20230607
LC record available at https://lccn.loc.gov/2023020965

Printed in China
RR Donnelley, Dongguan, China

10 9 8 7 6 5 4 3 2 1

To Mick. May you never stop climbing.

You know this mountain.

EVEREST.

Any serious, high-altitude climber has this mountain on their bucket list. Even those who'd rather gaze up at the clouds instead of climb in them sometimes wonder about the view from the top of the world. How *amazing* it must be.

If you knew a helicopter was waiting outside your home, this very moment, for you to see that view for yourself, would you get on board?

The helicopter would drop you off directly on the summit, and you could stay there for as long as you'd like, soaking in the view. It's just that easy.

It's the offer of a lifetime.

Except you already know
that isn't how it works.

Forget the cold. Forget the brutal glare of the sun. Within your first breath, you'd be in trouble. Because there isn't enough oxygen in the air to keep yourself alive for even two minutes.

And yet, every year, there are people who stand on Everest's summit, and they breathe in the beautiful air, and they live.

What makes the difference?

IT'S THE CLIMB.

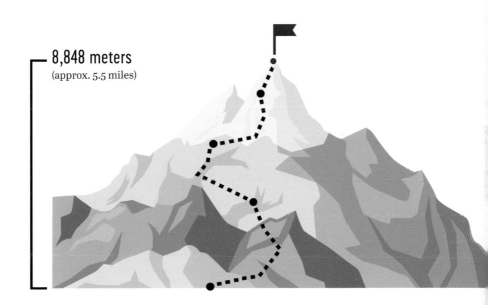

8,848 meters
(approx. 5.5 miles)

Everest rises roughly five and a half miles above sea level. For most hikers, five and a half miles is a good day's adventure. Yet climbers on Everest can spend up to *two months* on their journey.

The trek to base camp takes about ten days in each direction. Climbers remain there for three to six weeks while their bodies acclimate to the higher altitude, learning to generate more red blood cells capable of holding more oxygen.

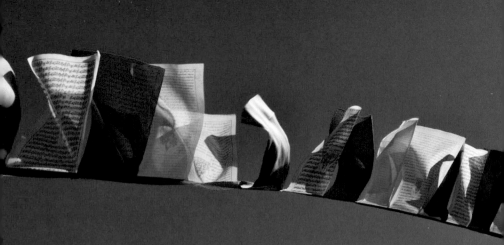

Even after the climbers begin the ascent, they spend time at each of the upper camps. Their bodies continue to change, day by day, until they can stand on top of the world, draw in a breath,

AND LIVE.

The climber does not change because they reached the summit. The climber reaches the summit because *they* changed.

That change comes with the climb.

Each of us is climbing to a summit of our own.
The summit is your dream, your goal—whatever
matters most to you.

Some dreams are bigger than others or more ambitious or more visible to the outside world. That doesn't make them more important.

Whatever your dream is, if it's *your* dream, then it's *your* summit.

You may have spent years staring up at that summit, wishing you had the time or money to pursue it. Maybe you are still waiting to feel "ready."

In Deuteronomy 2:3, the Lord says to Moses:

"Ye have compassed this mountain long enough. Turn you northward."

It can be easy to spend your time and energy staying busy with tasks that have no real meaning for you. That is circling the mountain—staying in motion but never moving toward your dreams. Remember, action does not always equal altitude.

For many people, north means *up*. So, consider this your call to get on the mountain.

BEGIN YOUR CLIMB.

Once you do, you'll notice other people are also climbing. They're steadily trekking uphill, their eyes trained upward in hopes of reaching their summit.

Many of those climbers are higher on the trail. Maybe they have better gear, or they seem to dance their way upward while you step aside to catch your breath, asking yourself why you even bother.

What's the point?

Fortunately, this is no ordinary mountain. Here, the ridge of endless trails leads to a vast number of summits.

So many, in fact, that whatever your dream might be, there is a summit specifically for *you*!

The other climbers are not your competitors. They have their own summit to reach. Their successes and failures will not impact your journey. Maybe you share the same trail now, but eventually the path will fork, and they'll turn in their own direction.

Or maybe they won't.

Yes, some climbers are headed to the same summit as you are. Maybe that doesn't matter. Some summits are wide enough to accommodate a crowd.

But some are narrow, with steep drop-offs. Those who occupy such narrow summits may look at you with suspicion, as if your arrival threatens to displace them.

Don't worry about them now. Simply focus on the five steps necessary to reaching *your* summit.

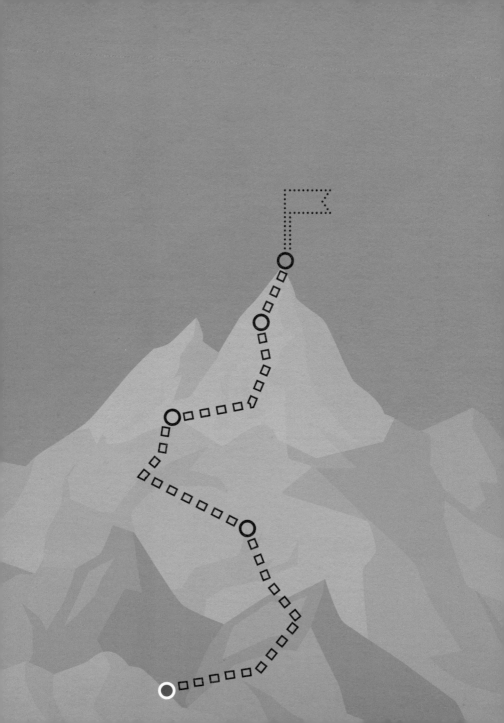

1

STEP ONE
Gear Up!

Your gear will be more complex than a coat, hat, and gloves. For this climb to succeed, you must protect your heart and mind and soul. This is not the time to be cheap, or to skimp on your supplies.

Instead, choose only the best for yourself, though it may be harder than you think. Here is your supply list:

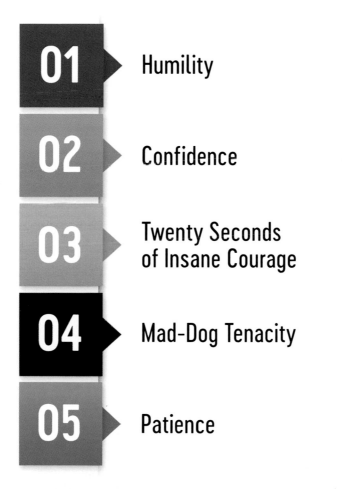

01 ▸ Humility

02 ▸ Confidence

03 ▸ Twenty Seconds of Insane Courage

04 ▸ Mad-Dog Tenacity

05 ▸ Patience

01 Humility

The adage is true: too much ego will kill talent. Humility allows us to remain teachable, and a teachable person asks for help along the trail.

They know that their position on the trail doesn't make them better or worse than anyone else.

Whatever your altitude, and no matter how fast or slow you advance on the trail, remain grateful that you get to do this amazing climb at all.

02 Confidence

Confidence doesn't mean you expect to accomplish your goal perfectly, or believe that success will come without struggles. Instead, it's the belief that when those struggles come, you will figure out a way to manage them—even if that solution is not readily apparent.

Confidence is the belief that you deserve success, even if others have done it better, even if you've failed before, and even if you still aren't sure what success will look like for you.

Finally, confidence is recognizing that you have done difficult things before, and that you can do difficult things again—even if you don't yet know what those difficult things will be.

03 Twenty Seconds of Insane Courage

Author Benjamin Mee said, "Sometimes all you need is twenty seconds of insane courage, and I promise you, something great will come of it."

It only takes twenty seconds to hit send on your résumé, or to make the phone call, or to say "yes" to an opportunity. Twenty seconds to raise your hand to take the first step. Twenty seconds to finish the final step and then ask, "What's next?"

You don't need enough courage right now for an entire lifetime of possibilities. Sometimes all you need is the courage to get you through the next twenty seconds. If that's all you can do, then it's enough.

04 Mad-Dog Tenacity

Often we feel as if a barricade sits between us and our dream, and that nothing we do will help us get around it. But there is always a way.

No matter how fierce the storm, you will outlast it. No matter how dark the night, you will see the dawn. No matter how distant the finish line, stay true to your values and keep going.

The universe responds to people who refuse to give up. Keep climbing, keep pushing against that barricade. It will break before you do.

05 Patience

All of these traits must be brought into balance with patience. There is a place on every climb to pause long enough to enjoy the view as you catch your breath. Travel at the right pace for you.

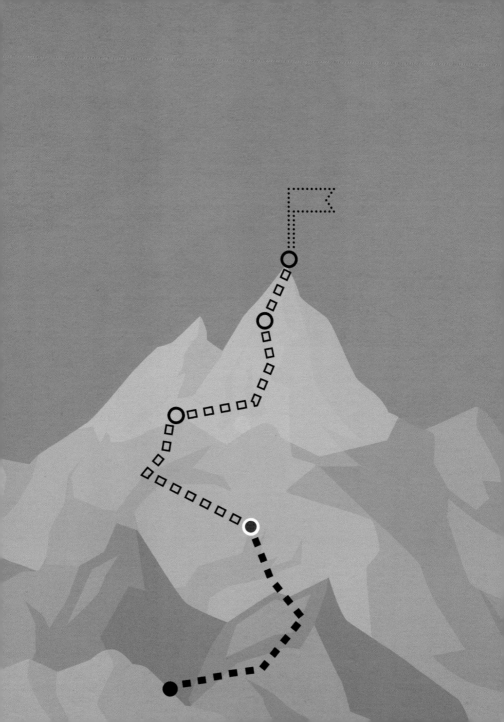

2

STEP TWO
Choose Your Climbing Team Carefully

Sometimes having the right team around you can make the difference between reaching your summit and only staring at it from below.

We all have many people in our lives, and we need them all for various reasons, but your climbing team should include four specific types of people.

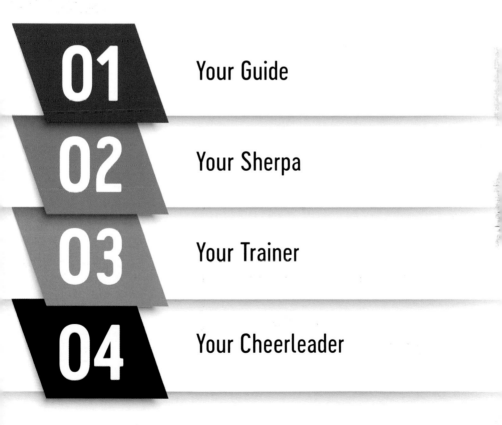

01 Your Guide

02 Your Sherpa

03 Your Trainer

04 Your Cheerleader

Your Guide.

This is your mentor. They've either been to your summit before or they're higher on the trail than you are, and they are willing to clear some hazards out of your way. Their job is to keep you from getting lost as you climb.

Your Sherpa.

These people can bear some of the weight of your climb, whether that is emotional, physical, or spiritual. Any climb is too difficult to manage alone. Ask for help when you need it. Accept help when it's offered.

Your Trainer.

While the guide walks ahead of you, the trainer stays at your side. They are there to teach you, so they won't always say what you want to hear. Listen anyway.

Your Cheerleader.

This is the person you call from your first step on the trail to the final step upon the summit, and at every checkpoint along the way. Even if they lack the technical expertise for your climb, they want you to succeed, and nobody will cheer louder when you do.

It's important to recognize that some of the people around you care about your success, but they don't fully understand what you're trying to accomplish. That's okay. They can love you from the sidelines. In short, your climbing team is made up of those who motivate, teach, or build you up.

Let go of any advice, any voice,
or any complaint that says
you cannot succeed.

There is no place for those ideas
during your climb, or in your life.

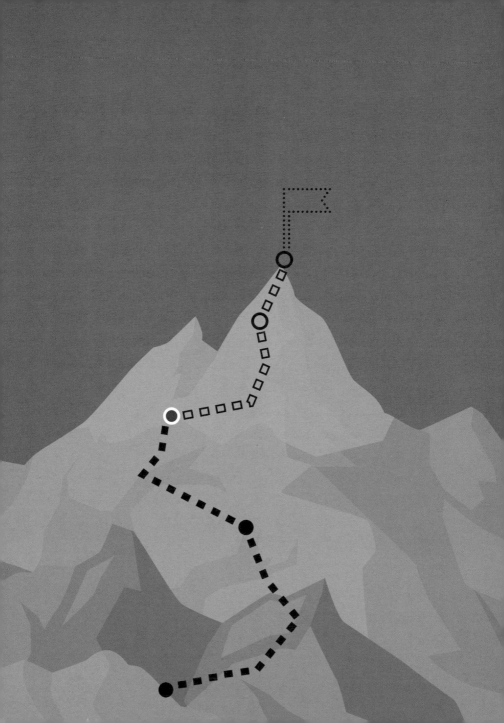

3

STEP THREE
Choose Your Route

The multi-summit mountain has many trails, but be warned: even if the trail seems to unfold in the direction you want to go, not all trails end at the same summit. Be sure that the route you choose is headed to *your* destination, not a cheap substitute with a paltry view. That might require you to abandon the smooth, flat trail for one with a steeper altitude and rocks in your way.

If it does, then know that this part of your climb can change you for the better. It can make you stronger, more determined, and more grateful for every step you achieve.

Keep climbing and eventually, you will reach your summit. The view will be wonderful. Celebrate that. Enjoy it. But, as your eyes turn upward, you may also realize something unexpected. There is another summit, higher on the mountain. You always vaguely knew it was there, but it felt too far away. Until now.

Now you realize your summit was simply base camp on the way to a new dream. And now you have the skills to continue climbing. So up you go, until achieving this new dream puts you in sight of yet another summit, another new goal.

This is the climb, and this is life.

This is how we continue to grow. If you stay in one place too long, with no new dreams or plans, then over time, the view will grow stagnant. Your muscles will soften.

That is also the reason you need not worry if the summit you are seeking is narrow and already occupied by others. Before long, they'll resume their climb with new dreams of their own, and space on your summit will open up.

THERE IS ALWAYS ROOM
FOR YOU TO SUCCEED.

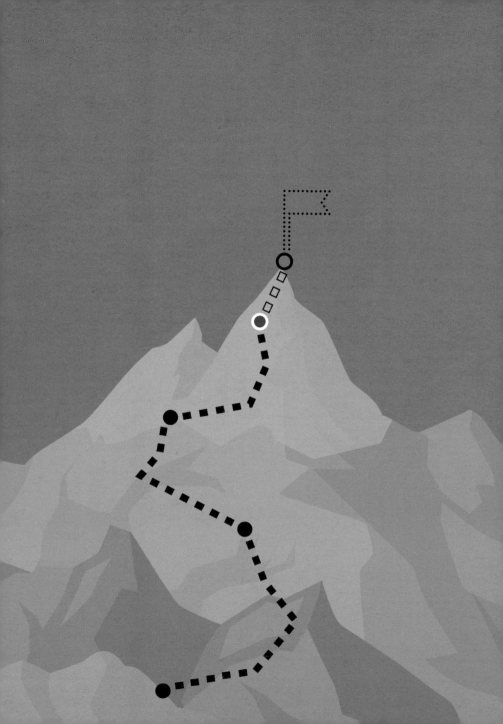

4

STEP FOUR
Cross the Crevasse

Every mountain has its share of crevasses.

Some gaps may run only an inch or two deep. Others may be so deep that you cannot see the bottom and so wide that you cannot hope to jump across.

On Everest, crevasses are crossed by laying a ladder horizontally along the gap, then stringing ropes across the sides for the climber to hold onto as they cross. They must put each foot down in the exact place on the rung, or they could lose their balance and fall.

We call such falls *failure*.

We all have our falls; we all experience failure. It's always painful, and for some, it's devastating.

But what matters most isn't the fall; it's what we tell ourselves about the fall.

If a climber on Everest fell into a crevasse, they would never tell themselves that they failed at their efforts, so now they must live the rest of their lives in that gap. Never.

But in life, we do that all the time. If we try and fail, sometimes we quit on our dream, choosing to live in the crevasse.

Perhaps you might feel that you are in such a place. But you always have a choice.

There is always a way to move forward.

HOW?

Every climber carries a strong rope on their climb because failure happens to all of us. Yet failure is not the end. Quitting is the end. Failure is simply your cue to find a way to reset, improve, and then try again. Keep hold of your rope, then call on your climbing team, and get yourself out of that hole.

We are not meant to
live in the crevasse.

WE ARE MEANT TO CLIMB.

5

STEP FIVE
Summit

Some days, all you can do is put one foot in front of the other. That's okay. Do that. Even if you advance only a few inches, at least you advanced.

If it's a rest day, then rest. That, too, is part of a successful climb. Let your body acclimate to every new elevation. But stay on the mountain. If you do that and keep your eye on your goal and continue to take steps forward, then reaching your summit becomes inevitable.

You can do this. You can.

The climb may not be easy, it may take longer than you think, and you may have much to learn along the way. It may require sacrifices of your time and energy. But the summit is there and waiting for you.

The day will come when you stand on *your* summit. The view will be extraordinary, so do not accept anything less.

Begin today. Dream your dreams, the biggest that you can imagine. Gear up, assemble your team, and choose your route.

Some people plan to begin climbing . . . one day.

For you, this is Day One!

Get on the mountain.

Take a deep breath.

YOUR SUMMIT IS WAITING.

PHOTO CREDITS

ABOUT THE AUTHOR

JENNIFER A. NIELSEN was born and raised in northern Utah. She is a #1 *New York Times* best-selling author of several series and novels, including The Ascendance series, beginning with *The False Prince*; the Traitor's Game series; the historical novels *Resistance*, *A Night Divided*, *Words on Fire*, *Rescue*, and several other titles. Jennifer has won multiple awards, including the Sydney Taylor Notable Book Award and several state book awards. She has been the keynote speaker at many writing and publishing conferences. Her message in *Once Upon a Climb* was originally written to inspire other writers to keep writing and doing those things to reach their own personal goals.

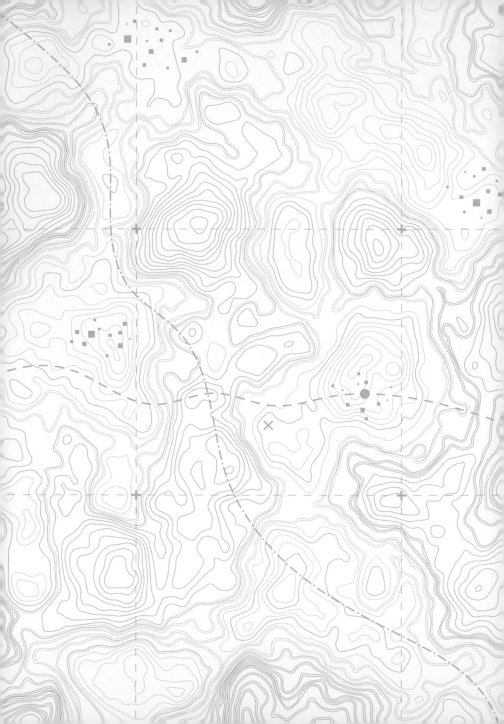